2|4|14

H
AN   S

Spilsbury, Louise

Louise and
Richard Spilsbury

D1335668

First published in this edition in 2011

Published by Evans Brothers Limited
2A Portman Mansions
Chiltern Street
London W1U 6NR

Produced for Evans Brothers Limited by
White-Thomson Publishing Ltd.,
+44 (0) 843 2087 460
www.wtpub.co.uk

Printed & bound in China by New Era Printing Co. Ltd.

Editor: Dereen Taylor
Consultants: Nina Siddall, Head of Primary School
Improvement, East Sussex; Norah Granger, former
primary head teacher and senior lecturer in Education,
University of Brighton
Designer: Leishman Design

British Library Cataloguing in Publication Data
Spilsbury, Louise
     Houses and Homes - (Start-up design
     and technology)
     1. Architecture, Domestic - Juvenile literature
     2. Dwellings
     I. Title II. Spilsbury, Louise
     728

ISBN: 978 0 237 54372 3

Acknowledgements:
Special thanks to the following for their help and
involvement in the preparation of this book:
Staff and pupils at Coldean Primary School, Brighton;
Elm Grove Primary School, Brighton and
Hassocks Infants School, Hassocks.

Picture Acknowledgements:
Chris Fairclough cover, 5 (right), 8, 9, 12 (right), 13, 14,
15, 19, 20, 21; Corbis 16, 17; Ecoscene 4 (bottom right);
Liz Price title page, 5 (left), 10, 11, 12 (left); Topfoto 7;
WTpix 4 (top and bottom left).

Artwork:
Emily Price age 5, page 6 (right); Tom Price age 8,
page 6 (left); Hattie Spilsbury age 10, pages 13 and 18.

Contents

Houses and homes

Jack's class is looking at different kinds of homes. There are terraced houses, blocks of flats, and detached houses near Jack's school.

What is the purpose of houses and homes?
Why do houses come in different designs?

 4   homes   terraced   houses   flats

What kind of home do you live in?

detached   purpose   designs

Outside and inside

Asha lives in an old cottage. Jess lives in a new terraced house. They have drawn pictures of their homes with labels for the different features.

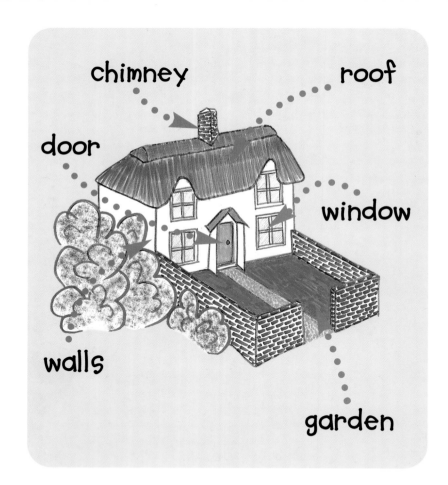

chimney

roof

door

window

walls

garden

chimney

roof

walls

door

window

How are the houses similar? How are they different?

cottage   labels   features

Can you match the words around the picture to the correct rooms in this doll's house?

bathroom   kitchen   hall

lounge   bedroom   dining room

Is it a model of an old house or a new house?
What rooms does your home have?

similar   rooms

Shapes and homes

Stefan drew a picture of his house on the computer.

He used the mouse to move different shapes across the screen. He made a house from circles, squares, rectangles and triangles.

computer   mouse

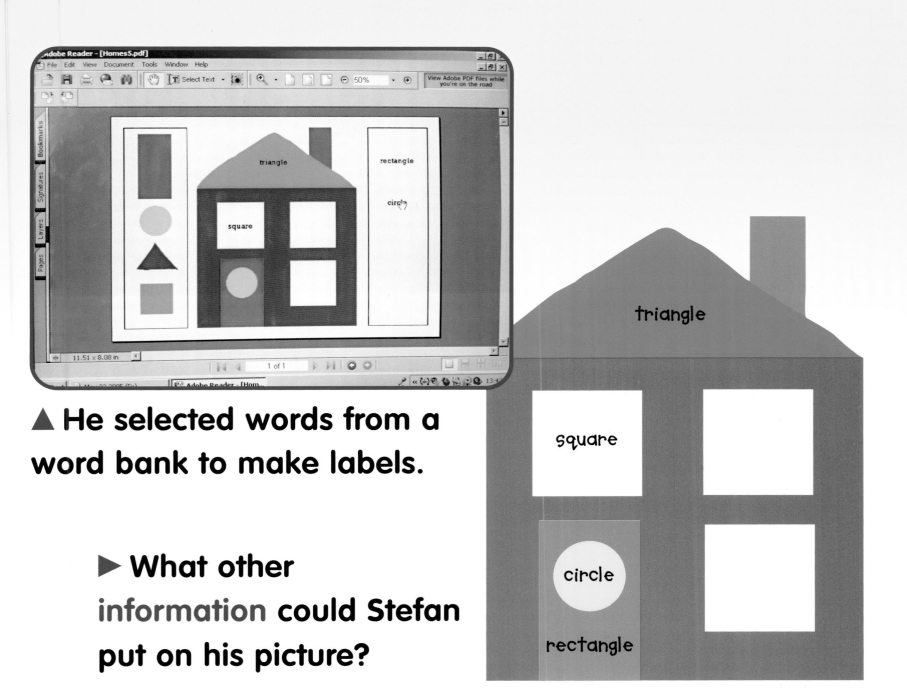

▲ He selected words from a word bank to make labels.

▶ What other information could Stefan put on his picture?

What kind of house would you make from shapes? Who would you design a house for?

screen   information

Making a house

Emily has been reading 'The Three Little Pigs'. She wants to make a **strong model** house for the pigs.

Would you make a **flat** roof with Lego boards like Emily, or a **steep** roof from folded cardboard?

10 **strong**   **model**   **flat**   **steep**

Emily tests her house.

▲ She rests a book on top to check the roof won't fall in.

▲ Emily's grandpa uses a hairdryer to check it won't blow down.

How can Emily test if the house is waterproof?

test   waterproof

Materials hunt

Emily looks at different materials in her home.

▲ The windows are made of glass. Glass is transparent.

▲ The roof is covered with stone tiles. They keep the rain out.

materials   glass   transparent

▼ **The front door is made of wood. Wood is strong.**

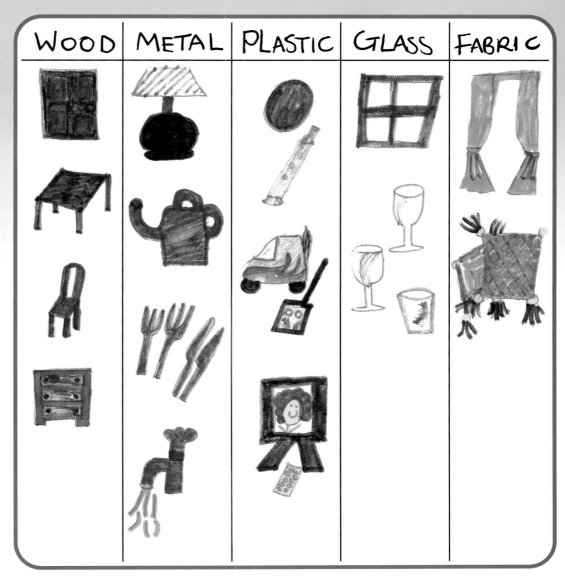

WOOD	METAL	PLASTIC	GLASS	FABRIC

▲ **Emily made a chart to group the different materials in her home. What other objects in your home could you add to this chart?**

Designing a bedroom

Tamika is making a bedroom for her dolls.

▲ Tamika writes a list of things that could go in the bedroom.

▲ She uses a box for her room and puts soft carpet on the floor. Tamika glues together two layers of card to make the table.

Why does Tamika use two layers of card for her table?

14

soft   glues

◀ **Tamika chooses the doll that is the right scale for the room.**

WARNING!
Scissors are sharp. Use them with care.

How could Tamika improve the bedroom? What kind of bedroom would you design for your best friend?

scale   improve   15

Homes around the world

Hassan's class is looking at homes around the world.

◀ **White walls keep homes cool in hot places.**

▶ **Steep roofs let melting snow slide off homes in cold places.**

◀ **Why is this house on stilts?**

▶ An **architect** designs **buildings**. The model is small but everything on it is built to scale.

Why would an architect make a model like this?

stilts   **architect**   **buildings**   **17**

Planning a model house

Josie is planning a model **bungalow** for her grandpa who cannot climb stairs. She draws her design and thinks about the materials she will use.

card shapes for tiles

plastic container for windows

hinge

fabric for curtains

split pin for door handle

Why do you think she chooses a split pin for the door handle?

bungalow   split pin

Josie tests different ways of making **hinges** for the door.

▲ She **scores** and **bends** card to make a hinge.

◄ She joins two pieces of card together with tape.

scores   bends   hinges   19

Making a model house

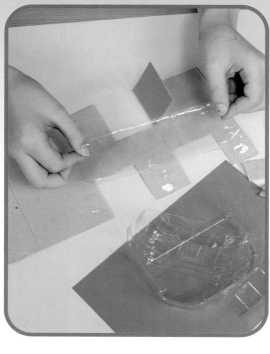

▲ Josie opens a cardboard box and cuts two windows. Then she cuts and bends the door.

▲ She sticks in the windows and the curtains.

▲ She sticks the box back together. Then she folds a piece of card for the roof and checks that it fits.

20 fits   decorated   evaluate

Josie has decorated her house. She asks Ben to evaluate her model.

The transparent windows work really well and I like the opening door.

Materials and tools
- cardboard box • paint • fabric
- coloured card • scissors • glue
- plastic container • split pin

Do you think Josie's house looks like her plan? Why do you think this is?

Further information for Parents and Teachers

HOUSES AND HOMES ACTIVITY PAGE

Use the activities on these pages to help you to make the most of *Houses and Homes*.

Activities suggested on this page support progression in learning by consolidating and developing ideas from the book and helping the children to link the new concepts with their own experiences. Making these links is crucial in helping young children to engage with learning and to become lifelong learners. Ideas on the next page develop essential skills for learning by suggesting ways of making links across the curriculum and in particular to literacy, mathematics and ICT.

WORD PANEL

Check that the children know the meaning of each of these words from the book.

- architect
- brick
- building
- bungalow
- cottage
- decorations
- design
- detached
- flats
- home
- house
- materials
- model
- room
- scale
- steep
- stone
- terraced
- tiles
- wood

WHERE DO WE LIVE?

Take the class for a walk in the vicinity of the school to look at where people live. Allow children to take digital cameras and clipboards for making notes, sketches and rubbings.

- Are all of the buildings the same? What's the same and what's different? Were they all built at the same time and out of the same material?
- Draw children's attention to windows in the buildings. Are they all the same? What makes some of them different?
- Back at school, go online and find websites which have photographs of different places in the UK. Find streets near you which have buildings that look different from those near the school. How are they different?
- Do any of the children have relations who live elsewhere? What are the buildings like there?

A HOUSE OR A HOME?

Help children to identify similarities and differences in the meanings of the words 'house' and 'home'.

- Give groups of children sugar paper and marker pens. On some pieces of paper write 'house' and on others write 'home'. Ask children to write ideas which you would want to include in a definition of each word.
- Create a Venn diagram based on the children's ideas. What is common to both words? What is implied by 'home' rather than 'house'?
- Use information in the Venn diagram to create a class definition of 'home' and of 'house'.

HOUSES ROUND THE WORLD

Help children to understand that houses around the world have many similarities – and often many differences too.

- Print or collect images of houses from around the world. Allow children to spend time looking at them and talking about them. Write on the back which country the houses are from.
- Ask pairs of children to select four different images. Challenge the children to find out as much as they can about the place each house is from – what is the weather like there? How do people pass their days? Are the people who live in houses like these rich or poor people?
- Children can collect information from text or pictures. Ask each pair to present a short report explaining what they found out. This could be in the form of a poster.

HOUSES AS SETTINGS

Many stories are based in or around houses or homes.

- Start a chart to which children can contribute as they come across stories. Agree what the columns in the chart should be e.g. type of house, who lives there, is it a house or home
- Talk about whether or not the setting is important in the story. Would changing the setting make the story different?
- In shared, guided and independent writing, create paragraphs about scary houses, houses at night, family houses, isolated cottages, splendid castles etc.

USING HOUSES AND HOMES FOR CROSS-CURRICULAR WORK.

As citizens in 21st-century Britain, it is important that children develop key competencies as

- successful learners
- confident individuals and
- responsible citizens.

Cross-curricular work is particularly beneficial in developing the thinking and learning skills that contribute to building these competencies because it encourages children to make links, to transfer learning skills and to apply knowledge from one context to another. As importantly, cross-curricular work can help children to understand how schoolwork links to their daily lives. For many children, this is a key motivation in becoming a learner.

The web below indicates some areas for cross-curricular study. Others may well come from your own class's engagement with the ideas in the book.

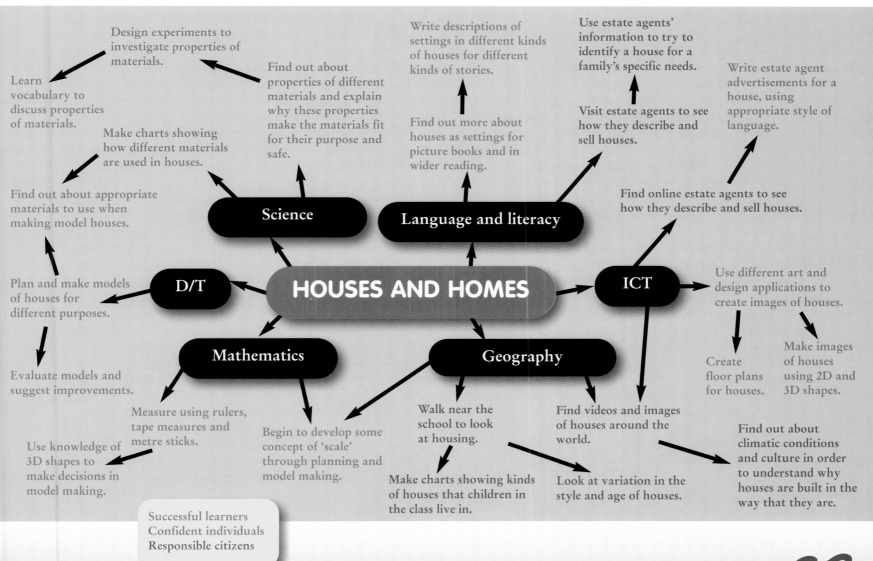

Design experiments to investigate properties of materials.

Learn vocabulary to discuss properties of materials.

Make charts showing how different materials are used in houses.

Find out about appropriate materials to use when making model houses.

Find out about properties of different materials and explain why these properties make the materials fit for their purpose and safe.

Write descriptions of settings in different kinds of houses for different kinds of stories.

Find out more about houses as settings for picture books and in wider reading.

Use estate agents' information to try to identify a house for a family's specific needs.

Visit estate agents to see how they describe and sell houses.

Write estate agent advertisements for a house, using appropriate style of language.

Find online estate agents to see how they describe and sell houses.

Science

Language and literacy

D/T

HOUSES AND HOMES

ICT

Mathematics

Geography

Plan and make models of houses for different purposes.

Evaluate models and suggest improvements.

Measure using rulers, tape measures and metre sticks.

Use knowledge of 3D shapes to make decisions in model making.

Begin to develop some concept of 'scale' through planning and model making.

Walk near the school to look at housing.

Make charts showing kinds of houses that children in the class live in.

Find videos and images of houses around the world.

Look at variation in the style and age of houses.

Use different art and design applications to create images of houses.

Create floor plans for houses.

Make images of houses using 2D and 3D shapes.

Find out about climatic conditions and culture in order to understand why houses are built in the way that they are.

Successful learners
Confident individuals
Responsible citizens

23

Index